# THE GARDEN
# WAY · OF · THE
# CROSS

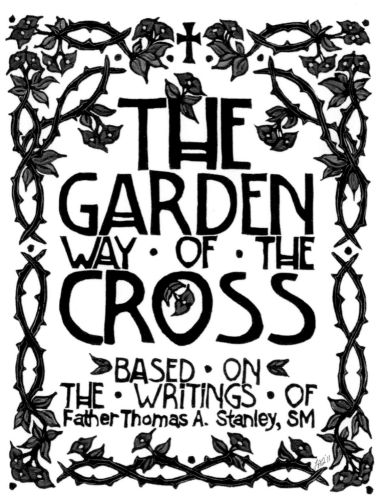

# THE GARDEN WAY · OF · THE CROSS

### BASED · ON · THE · WRITINGS · OF
### Father Thomas A. Stanley, SM

ILLUSTRATIONS BY Louise Tessier

NOVALIS

Book design by Martin Gould

Published by Novalis

Publishing Office
10 Lower Spadina Avenue, Suite 400
Toronto, Ontario, Canada
M5V 2Z2

Head Office
4475 Frontenac Street
Montréal, Québec, Canada
H2H 2S2

www.novalis.ca

**Library and Archives Canada Cataloguing in Publication**
Stanley, Thomas, 1921-
    The garden way of the cross / Thomas Stanley ; Louise Tessier, illustrator.

ISBN 978-2-89646-536-1

    1. Stations of the Cross--Meditations.  2. Stations of the Cross--Pictorial works.  I. Tessier, Louise  II. Title.

BX2040.S73 2013          232.96          C2013-901340-7

Printed in China.

We acknowledge the financial support of the Government of Canada through the Canada Book Fund for business development activities.

5  4  3  2  1      17  16  15  14  13

## THE QUIET GARDEN PRAYER

O Lord Jesus,
true gardener,
work in us what you want of us,
for without you we can do nothing.

For you are indeed the true gardener,
at once the maker and tiller
and keeper of your garden,
you who plant with the word,
water with the spirit
and give your increase with your power.

*Prayer of the twelfth-century Cistercian Guerric of Igny*

# Contents

# For Larry and Eric

## ACKNOWLEDGEMENTS

I wish to thank Father Thomas Stanley for generously granting me permission to use his writings as my inspiration, and Novalis for embracing my book proposal, especially Joseph Sinasac, for providing sincere counsel, Anne Louise Mahoney, for her guidance throughout the editing process, and Grace Deutsch, for her enthusiastic efforts on behalf of this book.

Ray Tessier and Brian Hudec gave me their professional advice and assistance, and I thank them for their support.

I am forever grateful to my devoted parents, George and Delores Hudec, who have been unwavering examples of what it is to live a Christian life. They fostered my God-given gifts along with those of my nine siblings. Growing up, my parents allowed us to go where the Spirit led us, particularly when it came to the arts. I thank them for encouraging a creative spirit in our very active home. I also recognize the encouragement and support of my other family members and all of my dear friends.

I especially acknowledge my husband, Larry, and my son, Eric, who have shown steadfast patience, understanding and love as I committed much time and energy to the fulfillment of this spiritual quest.

*Louise Tessier*
*February 2013*

---

We shall not cease from exploration,
and the end of all our exploring will be to arrive where we started
and know the place for the first time.

T.S. ELIOT

It all started with a garden. At least that's how I've come to see it.

When asked to write a foreword for the wonderful marriage of scripture, symbol and art you are holding in your hands, I was honoured. Not only was I appreciative of Fr. Stanley's meditations on the stations themselves, I was quite moved by and drawn to the beauty and skilled simplicity of Louise Tessier's flower illustrations. I was even more delighted to learn that Louise makes her home in Regina, Saskatchewan, for it was there that my love for plants and gardens was first awakened. I lived and worked at the Marian Centre from 1975 to 1980, and it seemed everyone we knew, whether they lived on a farm or in the city, had a garden. Our Chinese neighbours taught us to grow snow peas and when to pick them. We grew a few tender vegetables and every herb imaginable in a little fenced plot. The first maidenhair fern I ever saw was at a Ukrainian friend's house there. It was a marvel to me, so delicately splendid, although it was years before I would know its Marian symbolism. Louise's image of the maidenhair brought back that vivid memory.

It was there, too, that I learned about the healing properties and spiritual significance of plants and herbs. Some dear friends lent me a book on medieval monastic gardens that briefly described how certain monasteries would plant around the Lady Chapel flowers and herbs that had associations with the life and virtues of the Virgin Mary; another of the monks' gardens might be dedicated to plants that symbolized the life of Christ – his birth, suffering, death and resurrection. That knowledge planted a seed in my own heart, lying dormant until, many years later, a young landscape designer helped me design my own little garden. Imagine my surprise when he suggested a Mary Garden! I immediately said yes and got to work on researching which plants to include.

From there I started to correspond with a man who would become my mentor, John Stokes, cofounder of the Mary Garden movement in the United States, a historian of the movement, as well as a compiler of seemingly exhaustive lists of the botanical, common and religious names of plants to grow in one's own little Eden. After my garden and I were featured in a few newspapers, I began to teach about the significance of Mary Gardens and about the place of gardening in the life of the spirit.

In medieval times, a garden became a teaching tool for the unschooled. The common names of the flowers, plants and trees told of the virtues and life of Mary, and the story of Christ's passion. They were a poor person's catechism, a mnemonic of the divine.

There is so much to say about gardens. With time, my view of them has gotten both simpler and deeper. Humans have been creating gardens in one way or another, in most of our civilizations, since ancient times. Today, a garden is both personal and universal. It is a metaphor for many things – the earth, the soul, paradise. The *pairi daeza* of the Persians simply meant "enclosure" or "park." The Hebrews translated this as *pardes*, which, in the first translations of the Bible into Greek, became *paradeisos*. Eden was that paradise, the garden planted by the Lord God in Genesis. It is where we were created and where we were meant to live forever. That is, until our arrogance and eating from the Tree of the Knowledge of Good and Evil caused us to be cast out. Every garden we create is an attempt to go back to those gates that are forever guarded by angels with fiery swords and say, "We're sorry, we made a mistake. Let us back in."

Perhaps the most important thing we learn from the Eden story is that we are and always have been part of the picture. Paradise was created for us. And we are part of the created world. We are the dust, the stuff that Paradise was made from and for.

The Garden becomes a botanical sort of typology that sees the Tree of the Garden become the Tree of Jesse and eventually the Tree of the Cross. The Garden sees Eve, the mother of all who live and then die, become Mary, the Mother of God and of our salvation. As the ancient carol sings, "Nova, Nova, Ave fit ex Eva!" ("News, News, Mary [Ave Maria] has been made from Eve!") By giving birth to Christ, Mary, the "Garden Enclosed," redeems our humanity and becomes the new Eve. With the Resurrection, those closed gates of Eden become the stone that is rolled away from the tomb, letting us back into the Garden where we encounter the Risen Christ, almost mistaking him for the gardener.

Learning the stories, names, legends and symbolism of these familiar and common plants means that we may never spend time in a garden in quite the same way again.

*Lauretta Santarossa*

11

# Introduction

The fourteen scriptural Stations of the Cross follow the journey of Jesus from the Last Supper to his resurrection. The time-honoured tradition of praying the Stations of the Cross is a mini-pilgrimage to Jerusalem – a way of reflecting on the suffering of Jesus and sharing in it as we each carry our own daily cross. Meditations on the Stations of the Cross are often held during the season of Lent, as we prepare our hearts for the celebration of Easter, when Christ is raised from the dead, but we can pray them anytime.

As an artist, it has always been a goal of mine to produce work that reflects my Christian beliefs – either through the use of spiritual themes or by incorporating elements of nature into each design. During a sabbatical that began in 2009, I decided to take a more prayerful approach and focus solely on sacred art. I searched through my extensive files, which chronicle over a decade of production work, looking for a sacred or religious subject to explore. I was overjoyed when I happened upon Father Thomas Stanley's writings for The Garden Way of the Cross. His text, which follows the scriptural stations in a 1975 book entitled *The Way of the Cross* (written by Father Angelo Bonetti at the request of Pope Paul VI), connects scriptural verses to symbolic flowers and plants. Father Thomas wrote his text in 1993, when he was pastor at St. Catherine of Siena Parish in Portage, Michigan, where a garden had been planted in honour of the Virgin Mary.

His descriptive text, and the accompanying scripture passages, presented me with a new way of viewing the traditional Roman Catholic practice of reflecting on the suffering of Jesus. Instead of making traditional figurative plaques for the walls of a parish church, I set out to create ceramic tiles that would focus on botanical imagery. Father Thomas's text became a perfect fit for my artwork and a new focal point for prayer. With this novel approach, I envisioned The Garden Way of the Cross providing spiritual nourishment to Christians of all traditions, especially those who have an affinity for gardens and all living things.

After receiving Father Thomas's generous permission, I was inspired to spend the next two years designing and creating fifteen ceramic art tiles (an opening image and the fourteen stations). Like his text, they are entitled The Garden Way of the Cross. These tiles have become part of a group exhibition of sacred art ("Moved by the Spirit") that is making its way across North America. The seed of Father Thomas's writing was planted and grew into my exhibition. This book, which incorporates my fifteen designs as illustrations, is the harvest of this proverbial seed.

The process of creating these ceramic tiles began with my design on paper, which was transferred to linoleum printing blocks. The fifteen linoleum blocks were each hand carved and used to impress into slabs of clay. The clay slabs were then air dried, kiln fired, hand painted, varnished and framed.

As part of this extensive process (and for the purposes of the book illustrations), I used my studio printing press to transfer the ink images from the linoleum blocks to paper. I then embellished the prints with vibrant watercolour paints, giving life to the flowers and plants.

Through The Garden Way of the Cross, we journey along the botanical path with Jesus. The illustrations, with the repeated crown of thorns border on the first thirteen Stations, emphasize the suffering of Jesus as he made his way to his death. The tiny red flowers bursting forth from the spikes represent the blood that he shed. The fourteenth Station – Jesus Rises from the Dead – features Easter lilies to mark the resurrection. A prayerful focus on each illustration provides an uplifting way to meditate on both Father Thomas's text and these key scriptural passages.

In his infinite wisdom and through his magnificent botanical creation, God invites us, as he invited Jesus, into the perfect place for prayer – a garden.

*Louise Tessier*

## Praying The Garden Way of the Cross

---

> . . . the soul is a garden enclosed, our own perpetual paradise
> where we can be refreshed and restored.
>
> Thomas Moore

As you meditate on each station along The Garden Way of the Cross, imagine yourself walking slowly in a quiet garden. As you walk, take time – to be nourished by the scripture passages, to ponder the botanical reflections, and to gaze upon the illustrations, which together invite a hopeful approach to Jesus' sorrowful journey.

Scripture tells how Jesus retreated to the Garden of Gethsemani to pray. Amidst this quiet garden of prayer, may you find sanctuary – a place to be refreshed and restored.

*In the name of the Father, and of the Son, and of the Holy Spirit.*
*Amen.*

### Opening Prayer

---

*Heavenly Father, we pause from the cares and concerns of our daily*
*lives to spend a few moments reflecting upon the events surrounding*
*the death and resurrection of our Lord Jesus. Send your spirit into our*
*hearts, increase our faith and deepen our hope in the resurrection.*
*We ask this in the name of Jesus. Amen.*

JESUS AT THE LAST SUPPER

# Jesus at the Last Supper

*We adore you, O Christ, and we praise you.*
*Because by your holy cross, you have redeemed the world.*

When it was evening, he took his place with the twelve; and while they were eating, he said, "Truly I tell you, one of you will betray me." Judas, who betrayed him, said, "Surely not I, Rabbi?" He replied, "You have said so." While they were eating, Jesus took a loaf of bread, and after blessing it he broke it, gave it to the disciples, and said, "Take, eat; this is my body." Then he took a cup, and after giving thanks he gave it to them, saying, "Drink from it, all of you; for this is my blood of the covenant, which is poured out for many for the forgiveness of sins." (Matthew 26:20-28)

Consider the **Maidenhair Fern** (*Adiatum capillis-veneris*), a Mary flower often used in England to decorate the altar for the feast of Corpus Christi, which honours the Eucharist. Recall the woman who washed Christ's feet with her tears and dried them with her hair; then ponder the example of Christ washing the feet of his disciples, asking that they do as he did.

*Lord Jesus, help us to walk in your garden of charity,*
*placing the needs of others before our own.*

·II·

JESUS PRAYS IN THE GARDEN

# Jesus Prays in the Garden of Gethsemani

---

*We adore you, O Christ, and we praise you.*
*Because by your holy cross, you have redeemed the world.*

He came out and went, as was his custom, to the Mount of Olives;
and the disciples followed him. Then he withdrew from them about
a stone's throw, knelt down, and prayed, "Father, if you are will-
ing, remove this cup from me; yet, not my will but yours be done."
Then an angel from heaven appeared to him and gave him strength.
In his anguish he prayed more earnestly, and his sweat became like
great drops of blood falling down on the ground. (Luke 22:39-44)

Consider the **St. John's Wort** (*Hypericum perforatum*), named
"**Christ's Sweat**" from the blood-like red speckles dot-
ting its yellow petals. Consider also the **Wood Sorrel** (*Oxalis
acetosella*), a bitter Mary flower which, together with other bitter
herbs, symbolizes the bitterness of our Lord's passion and the
depth of our Lady's sorrows. The triple leaf of this plant suggests the Trinitarian scene in Gethsemani – the Son praying to
his Father and sustained by the Spirit in his agony. The sorrel's
white flower, stained with purple, suggests the passion of Christ,
the innocent victim.

*Lord Jesus, help us to walk in your garden of faith*
*when we do not understand.*

·III·

JESUS IS TAKEN PRISONER

# Jesus is Taken Prisoner

*We adore you, O Christ, and we praise you.*
*Because by your holy cross, you have redeemed the world.*

While Jesus was still speaking, Judas, one of the twelve, arrived; and with him there was a crowd with swords and clubs, from the chief priests, the scribes, and the elders. Now the betrayer had given them a sign, saying, "The one I will kiss is the man; arrest him and lead him away under guard." So when he came, he went up to him at once and said, "Rabbi!" and kissed him. Then they laid hands on him and arrested him. (Mark 14:43-46)

Consider the **Mistletoe** (*Viscum album*), or **Christ's Cross**. There is something very striking about the fresh golden-green leaves and white waxen berries of this plant as they spring from a tree in death-like winter sleep. It suggested to Marian devotees the Christ-flowering from the root of Jesse that took place in Mary's womb after an Old Testament winter of expectant waiting. The mistletoe was formerly used in church decoration, and it is thought that the custom of kissing under the mistletoe originated in the ceremonial "kiss of peace" at the Christ Mass, a striking contrast to the kiss of Judas.

*Lord Jesus, help us to walk in your garden of courage*
*when we are afraid.*

·IV·

JESUS IS BROUGHT
BEFORE THE SANHEDRIN

# Jesus is Brought Before the Sanhedrin

*We adore you, O Christ, and we praise you.*
*Because by your holy cross, you have redeemed the world.*

They took Jesus to the high priest. Then the high priest stood up before them and asked Jesus, "Have you no answer? What is it that they testify against you?" But he was silent and did not answer. Again the high priest asked him, "Are you the Messiah, the Son of the Blessed One?" Jesus said, "I am; and 'you will see the Son of Man seated at the right hand of the Power', and 'coming with the clouds of heaven.'" Then the high priest tore his clothes and said, "Why do we still need witnesses? You have heard his blasphemy! What is your decision?" All of them condemned him as deserving death. (Mark 14:60-64)

Consider the **Yellow Iris** (*Iris sp.*), or **Mary's Sword of Sorrow**, from its sword-like foliage recalling the prophecy of Simeon to Mary at the Presentation of the child Jesus in the Temple – that Jesus would be a sign that would be contradicted, and Mary's own soul would be pierced by a sword, "that the thoughts of many hearts will be revealed." Consider also the **Lungwort** (*Pulmonaria officinalis*), also known as **The Virgin Mary's Tears** or **Our Lady's Milk Herb**. The leaves of this Mary plant are handsomely blotched and speckled with white. When it blossoms, pink buds open into blue flowers. It is said that Mary, on her way out of Jerusalem after presenting Jesus in the Temple, sat down to nurse him. This plant at her feet caught the blue of her eye, but the plant grew pink when Mary's eyes reddened with weeping as she reflected on the sufferings predicted for her son. The baby moved suddenly and some of her milk fell on the leaves, causing the white markings that we still find on them.

*Lord Jesus, help us to walk in your garden of justice*
*in order to help the oppressed.*

V.

JESUS IS DENIED BY PETER

## The Fifth Station:
# Jesus is Denied by Peter

*We adore you, O Christ, and we praise you.*
*Because by your holy cross, you have redeemed the world.*

While Peter was below in the courtyard, one of the servant-girls said, "You also were with Jesus, the man from Nazareth." But he denied it. Then the cock crowed. And the servant-girl, on seeing him, began again to say to the bystanders, "This man is one of them." But again he denied it. Then after a little while the bystanders again said to Peter, "Certainly you are one of them; for you are a Galilean." But he began to curse, and he swore an oath, "I do not know this man you are talking about." At that moment the cock crowed for the second time. (Mark 14:66-72)

Consider the **Passionflower** (*Passiflora sp.*) whose ten petals were seen to symbolize the twelve apostles, less Judas who betrayed and Peter who denied. A **Passionflower vine** *(Passiflora Incarnata)* presents multiple symbols:

~ the spiralled tendrils represent the Lash of Christ's scouring;
~ the central flower column represents the Pillar of the Scourging;
~ the radial filaments represent the Crown of Thorns;
~ the stigma represents the Nails;
~ the anthers represent the Wounds;
~ the style represents the Sponge used to moisten Christ's lips with vinegar;
~ the leaves represent the head of the Centurion's spear;
~ the red stains represent Christ's blood drops;
~ the round fruit represents the World Christ came to save; and
~ the fragrance represents the Spices prepared by the Holy Women.

*Lord Jesus, help us to walk in your garden of truth*
*to speak for what is right.*

·VI·

JESUS IS TAKEN TO PILATE

# THE SIXTH STATION:
## Jesus is Taken to Pilate

---

*We adore you, O Christ, and we praise you.*
*Because by your holy cross, you have redeemed the world.*

Then they took Jesus from Caiaphas to Pilate's headquarters. Then Pilate asked him, "Are you the King of the Jews?" Jesus answered, "Do you ask this on your own, or did others tell you about me?" Pilate replied, "I am not a Jew, am I? Your own nation and the chief priests have handed you over to me. What have you done?" Jesus answered, "My kingdom is not from this world. If my kingdom were from this world, my followers would be fighting to keep me from being handed over to the Jews. But as it is, my kingdom is not from here." (John 18:33–36)

Consider the **Sundew** (*Drosera rotundifolia*). This plant has a rosette of green leaves thickly covered with red hairs, and on the tip of each hair is a drop of dew. It is also called **Gideon's Fleece**, which is a symbol of the Incarnation achieved in Mary's womb. This sign (a fleece dampened by dew while the ground all around was dry) was an answer to a prayer. Pilate, too, seeks a sign, but does not recognize the sign that God gives him. Mary always recognized God's signs.

*Lord Jesus, help us to walk in your garden of discernment,*
*recognizing God's plan for us.*

·VII·

JESUS IS SCOURGED
AND CROWNED WITH THORNS

# Jesus is Scourged and Crowned with Thorns

*We adore you, O Christ, and we praise you.*
*Because by your holy cross, you have redeemed the world.*

So Pilate, wishing to satisfy the crowd, released Barabbas for them; and after flogging Jesus, he handed him over to be crucified. Then the soldiers led him into the courtyard of the palace and they clothed him in a purple cloak; and after twisting some thorns into a crown, they put it on him. And they began saluting him, "Hail, King of the Jews!" They struck his head with a reed, spat upon him, and knelt down in homage to him. (Mark 15:15-19)

Consider the **Crown of Thorns** (*Euphorbia splendens*), or **Christ's Crown**, whose intense tiny red flowers brought to mind the blood drops emerging from Christ's forehead at the thorn-pricks. Then consider **Black Bryony** (*Tamus communis*), or **Our Lady's Seal**. The rootstock of this plant has great efficacy when crushed and spread in a medicinal plaster and applied to seal up a scar or bruise. It is known to be helpful in healing wounds – even in mending broken bones. How Mary must have wished to apply such a seal to the wounds of her son.

*Lord Jesus, help us to walk in your garden of strength*
*in order to bear our own suffering.*

VIII

JESUS IS CONDEMNED TO DEATH

# Jesus is Condemned to Death

*We adore you, O Christ, and we praise you.*
*Because by your holy cross, you have redeemed the world.*

But when Jesus was accused by the chief priests and elders, he did not answer. Then Pilate said to him, "Do you not hear how many accusations they make against you?" But he gave him no answer, not even to a single charge…. Now at the festival the governor was accustomed to release a prisoner for the crowd, anyone whom they wanted. And they said, "Barabbas." So he released Barabbas for them; and after flogging Jesus, he handed him over to be crucified. (Matthew 27:12-15, 20-21, 26)

Consider the **Lily of the Valley** (*Convallaria majalis*), also called **Our Lady's Tears**. This flower is said to have had its origin at the moment when Christ was condemned to death, for it was then that Mary wept; as her tears touched the earth, these flowers sprang up.

*Lord Jesus, help us to walk in your garden of acceptance*
*in times of great sorrow.*

·IX·

JESUS WITH SIMON OF CYRENE
MEETS THE WOMEN OF JERUSALEM

# Jesus with Simon of Cyrene
# Meets the Women of Jerusalem

*We adore you, O Christ, and we praise you.*
*Because by your holy cross, you have redeemed the world.*

As they led him away, they seized a man, Simon of Cyrene, who was coming from the country, and they laid the cross on him, and made him carry it behind Jesus. A great number of the people followed him, and among them were women who were beating their breasts and wailing for him. But Jesus turned to them and said, "Daughters of Jerusalem, do not weep for me, but weep for yourselves and for your children. For the days are surely coming when they will say to the mountains, 'Fall on us'; and to the hills, 'Cover us.' For if they do this when the wood is green, what will happen when it is dry?" (Luke 23:26-31)

Consider the **Ground Ivy** (*Nepeta glechoma*), which is also called **Where-God-Has-Walked** and **Madonna's Herb**. There are bright splashes of colour wherever it grows in large patches along country hedges and on waste ground. Its leaves are heart shaped, and its shoots, stem and leaf are of various shades of red and purple. Its labiate flowers, which grow out of the stem, are usually purple, but also sometimes white. It is a lovely reminder that God did walk this earth, even to Calvary, where he died for us. Consider the **Tiger Flower** (*Tigridia pavonia*) or **Christ's Knee**, symbol of Christ's bloodied knees from his falls while carrying the Cross.

*Lord Jesus, help us to walk in your garden of charity*
*to help others in need.*

JESUS IS CRUCIFIED

## The Tenth Station:
# Jesus is Crucified

*We adore you, O Christ, and we praise you.*
*Because by your holy cross, you have redeemed the world.*

Then they brought Jesus to the place called Golgotha (which means the place of a skull). It was nine o'clock in the morning. The inscription of the charge against him read, "The King of the Jews." And with him they crucified two bandits. Those who passed by derided him, shaking their heads and saying, "Aha! You who would destroy the temple and build it in three days, save yourself, and come down from the cross!" In the same way the chief priests, along with the scribes, were also mocking him. (Mark 15:22-31)

Consider the **Violet** (*Viola odorata*), also called **Our Lady's Modesty** or **Humility.** It is said to be among the flowers on which the shadow of the cross fell on the day of the crucifixion. The violet dropped its head in sorrow and in acknowledgement of the import of this great event, and its head has always remained downturned. The violet's colour suggests the purple of the Church in mourning. Consider also **Ladies' Tresses** (*Spiranthes cernua*), formerly known as **Our Lady's Tresses.** It takes this name from the spiral of its flower heads, reminiscent of plaited hair, and is associated with the legend that Mary, at the foot of the cross and in deep agony, tore out a tress of her hair, which St. John thereafter preserved.

*Lord Jesus, help us to walk in your garden*
*of mercy and forgiveness.*

XI

INRI

JESUS DIES ON THE CROSS

# Jesus Dies on the Cross

*We adore you, O Christ, and we praise you.*
*Because by your holy cross, you have redeemed the world.*

Then Jesus said, "Father, forgive them; for they do not know what they are doing." Meanwhile, standing near the cross of Jesus were his mother, and his mother's sister, Mary the wife of Clopas, and Mary Magdalene. When Jesus saw his mother and the disciple whom he loved standing beside her, he said to his mother, "Woman, here is your son." Then he said to the disciple, "Here is your mother." And from that hour the disciple took her into his own home. And about three o'clock Jesus cried with a loud voice, "Eli, Eli, lema sabachthani?" that is, "My God, my God, why have you forsaken me?" Then Jesus cried again with a loud voice and breathed his last. (Luke 23:34; John 19:25-27; Matthew 27:46, 50)

Consider the **Red Poppy** (*Papaver rhoeas*), or **Christ's Blood**. The flowers were said to have sprung up at the foot of the cross from the blood shed by Jesus. The poppy has long been seen as a flower of remembrance. Consider also the **Snowdrop** (*Galanthus nivalus*). It is said that when our first parents, Adam and Eve, were banished from Eden, they found winter beyond its gates. Eve stood sobbing, broken-hearted … the leafless trees, the bare ground and the biting winds were a dreadful contrast to the bowers of the garden of pleasure. God sent an angel to comfort her. The angel pointed to the ground, where her tears of penitence had fallen, and lo! There sprang up a little plant with a teardrop for its blossom. The angel gave the blossom to Eve, telling her that it was an assurance that happiness would return to her and all her progeny (offspring). The death and resurrection of Christ fulfills the promise of the snowdrop.

*Lord Jesus, help us to walk in your garden of empathy*
*for those who mourn.*

·XII·

INRI

JESUS' SIDE
IS PIERCED BY A LANCE·

## The Twelfth Station:
# Jesus' Side is Pierced by a Lance

*We adore you, O Christ, and we praise you.*
*Because by your holy cross, you have redeemed the world.*

They asked Pilate to have the legs of the crucified men broken and the bodies removed. But when they came to Jesus and saw that he was already dead, they did not break his legs. Instead, one of the soldiers pierced his side with a spear, and at once blood and water came out. These things occurred so that the scripture might be fulfilled, "None of his bones shall be broken." And again another passage of scripture says, "They will look on the one whom they have pierced." (John 19:31-37)

Consider the **Bleeding Heart** (*Dicentra spectabilis*), long associated with the suffering hearts of Jesus and Mary, and thus known both as **Christ's Heart** and also as **Mary's Heart**. Each of the pendant heart-shaped blooms has at its base a red-and-white droplet, which signifies the mixture of blood and water flowing from Christ's pierced side.

*Lord Jesus, help us to walk in your garden of trust*
*in times of confusion.*

XII

JESUS IS BURIED

# Jesus is Buried

*We adore you, O Christ, and we praise you.*
*Because by your holy cross, you have redeemed the world.*

Now there was a good and righteous man named Joseph. He came from the Jewish town of Arimathea, and he was waiting expectantly for the kingdom of God. This man went to Pilate and asked for the body of Jesus. Then he took it down, wrapped it in a linen cloth, and laid it in a rock-hewn tomb where no one had ever been laid. The women who had come with him from Galilee followed, and they saw the tomb and how his body was laid. Then they returned, and prepared spices and ointments. (Luke 23:50-56)

Consider the **Rosemary** (*Rosmarinus*). Legend says that the rosemary has been aromatic and evergreen since the time the swaddling clothes of the Holy Infant were hung upon it, and that since the time of Jesus' death, the rosemary has borne purple markings upon its lavender flowerets in memory of Calvary. In olden times, it was customary to strew rosemary on the tombs of the departed.

*Lord Jesus, help us to walk in your garden of hope*
*in the promise of the resurrection.*

·XIV·

JESUS RISES FROM THE DEAD
ALLELUIA

# Jesus Rises from the Dead. Alleluia!

*We adore you, O Christ, and we praise you.*
*Because by your holy cross, you have redeemed the world.*

After the sabbath, as the first day of the week was dawning, Mary Magdalene and the other Mary went to see the tomb. And suddenly there was a great earthquake; for an angel of the Lord, descending from heaven, came and rolled back the stone and sat on it. His appearance was like lightning, and his clothing white as snow. For fear of him the guards shook and became like dead men. But the angel said to the women, "Do not be afraid; I know that you are looking for Jesus who was crucified. He is not here; for he has been raised, as he said. Come, see the place where he lay." (Matthew 28:1-6)

Consider the **Tansy** (*Tanacetum vulgare*). Its hard golden flowerets will keep their colour for a long time if dried when they are at their best. Perhaps it is from this everlasting quality that it gets its name, tansy, for it is a word derived from *athanatos* (the Greek word for immortality). Its health-giving properties may also have inspired its name. In Europe it is called **Jesus-wort**. Consider also the **Resurrection Plant** (*Anastatica hierochuntica*), or **Rose of Jericho**, which was brought to Europe from the Holy Land by the Crusaders. After flowering, the Resurrection Plant dries up, but when soaked in water, it opens up again. Today, the **Easter Lily** (*Lilium longiflorum*) is widely valued as a symbol of Christ's resurrection. The striking trumpet-shaped white flowers announce the hope of new life through the resurrection and all the joy that the Easter Season brings. Alleluia!

*Lord Jesus, help us to walk in your garden of gratitude,*
*for through your triumph, we rejoice!*

## Closing Prayer

*Heavenly Father,*
*may we who have meditated on the death and resurrection of Jesus*
*following The Garden Way of the Cross*
*be filled with the hope and the joy of Jesus' life.*
*Confident of his presence among us*
*and of his power to touch us, to teach us,*
*to heal us and to forgive us,*
*may we have the strength and the power*
*to bring his love and his peace to all the people we meet.*
*We ask this in the name of Jesus,*
*who is our Lord forever and ever. Amen.*

*In the name of the Father, and of the Son, and of the Holy Spirit.*
*Amen.*

# GLOSSARY OF FLOWER NAMES

**Black Bryony** *(Tamus communis)* or **Our Lady's Seal** – *Seventh Station*

**Bleeding Heart** *(Dicentra spectabilis)* or **Christ's Heart** and also **Mary's Heart** – *Twelfth Station*

**Crown of Thorns** *(Euphorbia splendens)* or **Christ's Crown** – *depicted in the border of Stations One to Thirteen*

**Easter Lily** *(Lilium longiflorum)* – *depicted in the border of the Fourteenth Station*

**Ground Ivy** *(Nepeta glechoma)* or **Madonna's Herb** and also **Where-God-Has-Walked** – *Ninth Station*

**Ladies' Tresses** *(Spiranthes cernua)*, formerly **Our Lady's Tresses** – *Tenth Station*

**Lily of the Valley** *(Convallaria majalis)* or **Our Lady's Tears** – *Eighth Station*

**Lungwort** *(Pulmonaria officinalis)* or **The Virgin Mary's Tears** and also **Our Lady's Milk Herb** – *Fourth Station*

**Maidenhair Fern** *(Adiatum capillis-veneris)* – *First Station*

**Mistletoe** *(Viscum album)* or **Christ's Cross** – *Third Station*

**Passionflower** *(Passiflora sp.)* – *Fifth Station*

**Passionflower vine** *(Passiflora Incarnata)* – *Fifth Station*

**Red Poppy** *(Papaver rhoeas)* or **Christ's Blood** – *Eleventh Station*

**Resurrection Plant** *(Anastatica hierochuntica)* or **Rose of Jericho** – *Fourteenth Station*

**Rosemary** *(Rosmarinus)* or **Mary's Nosegay** – *Thirteenth Station*

**Snowdrop** *(Galanthus nivalus)* or **Candlemas Bells** and also **Purification Flowers** – *Eleventh Station*

**St. John's Wort** *(Hypericum perforatum)* or **Christ's Sweat** – *Second Station*

**Sundew** *(Drosera rotundifolia)* or **Gideon's Fleece** – *Sixth Station*

**Tansy** *(Tanacetum vulgare)* or **Jesus-Wort** – *Fourteenth Station*

**Tiger Flower** *(Tigridia pavonia)* or **Christ's Knee** – *Ninth Station*

**Violet** *(Viola odorata)* or **Our Lady's Modesty** and also **Our Lady's Humility** – *Tenth Station*

**Wood Sorrel** *(Oxalis acetosella)* – *Second Station*

**Yellow Iris** *(Iris sp.)* or **Mary's Sword of Sorrow** – *Fourth Station*